¿Cuantos Perros?
How Many Dogs?

Written by Bam Schildkraut

Illustrated by Steven Katz

¿Cuantos Perros? How Many Dogs?

Written By Bam Schildkraut

Illustrated by Steven Katz

Published by
Operation Outreach-USA Press
Holliston, MA

ISBN 978-0-9792144-6-2

Printed in the United States of America

Para Maya, Cole y los perros con amor.

For Maya, Cole and the dogs with love.

1 Uno, One.
Uno, One.

Un perro loves to run.

2 **Dos, Two.**
Dos, Two.

Dos perros tug an old shoe.

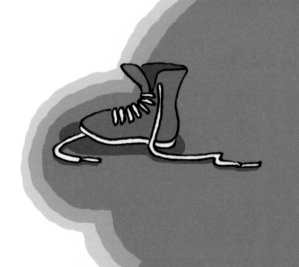

3 Tres, Three.

Tres, Three.

Tres perros dig by a tree.

4 **Cuatro, Four.**
Cuatro, Four.

Cuatro perros roll on the floor.

5 **Cinco, Five.**
Cinco, Five.
Cinco perros paddle and dive.

6 **Seis, Six.**

Seis, Six.

Seis perros play with sticks.

7 **Siete, Seven.**

Siete, Seven.

Siete perros lunch at eleven.

8 Ocho, Eight.

Ocho, Eight.

Ocho perros wait by the gate.

9 Nueve, Nine.

Nueve, Nine.

Nueve perros march in line.

10 **Diez, Ten.**

Diez, Ten.

Diez perros nap with a friend.

UNO DOS TRES CUATRO CINCO

SEIS   SIETE   OCHO   NUEVE   DIEZ

ONE   TWO   THREE   FOUR   FIVE

SIX SEVEN EIGHT NINE TEN

About Operation Outreach – USA

Operation Outreach – USA (OO-USA) provides free literacy and character education programs to elementary and middle schools across the country.

Because reading is the gateway to success, leveling the learning field for at-risk children is critical. By giving books to students to own, confidence is built and motivated readers are created. OO-USA selects books with messages that teach compassion, respect and determination. OO-USA involves the school and the home with tools for teachers and parents to nurture and guide children as they learn and grow.

More than one million children in schools in all fifty states have participated in the program thanks to the support of a broad alliance of corporate, foundation and individual sponsors.

To learn more about Operation Outreach – USA and how to help, visit www.oousa.org, call 1-800-243-7929 or email jgolden@oousa.org.